What Is Spiritual Warfare?

Basics of the Reformed Faith

Also available in the series:

What Is Spiritual Warfare?

STANLEY D. GALE

P&R
PUBLISHING
P.O. BOX 817 • PHILLIPSBURG • NEW JERSEY 08865-0817

Scripture quotations are from The Holy Bible, English Standard Version, copyright © 2001 by Crossway Bibles, a division of Good News Publishers. Used by permission. All rights reserved.

Italics within Scripture quotations indicate emphasis added.

Page design by Tobias Design

Printed in the United States of America

Library of Congress Cataloging-in-Publication Data

Gale, Stanley D., 1953–
  What is spiritual warfare? / Stanley D. Gale.
    p. cm. — (Basics of the Reformed faith)
  Includes bibliographical references.
  ISBN 978-1-59638-123-0 (pbk.)
  1. Spiritual warfare. 2. Reformed Church—Doctrines. I. Title.
  BV4509.5.G34 2008
  235'.4—dc22
                              2008023440

■Sunday morning, 6:00—I awakened to the last day of our family vacation. Every year we look forward to our time at the New Jersey shore to spend a week at Harvey Cedars Bible Conference on Long Beach Island—meals provided, daily Bible teaching, time with friends, things for the whole family to do, wholesome and relaxed atmosphere, sun and fun on the beach. But the week's stay was coming to its inevitable close. After the 11:00 a.m. worship service our family would head home with all the other revelers to return to the rigors of real life.

I decided to take the half-mile stroll from our restored Victorian hotel to the ocean. The unseasonably crisp day, especially for early August, reigned spectacular with its brilliant sun and bright blue, cloudless sky—a banquet for the senses.

As I walked, I took it all in, enjoying sweet communion with my God. My heart swelled with awe and wonder. My thoughts filled with praise, at various points compelled to adoration, driven to confession, overflowing with thanksgiving. I reached the beach and stepped over the crest of the sand dunes. That's when the sensory stimulation reached overload. The vast ocean spread out before me, the radiance of the sun magnified in reflection off its surface.

Sometimes the ocean can be restless, even violent, its waters gray and ominous, the surf raging with fury. Not today. The ocean rested as placid as I had ever seen it, the waters tranquil, generating waves no greater than the bay on the west side of the barrier island on which we stayed. A couple of beachcombers preceded my arrival, but their presence only contributed to the serenity of the scene. I gave glory to God as the Maker of the sea and all that is in it. To look upon it all, anyone would think there was not a care or worry in the world.

Appearances can be deceiving.

SEEING THE UNSEEN

A biblical worldview informs us that there is more to life than meets the eye. Contrary to a naturalistic world-view that denies the supernatural and insists on reality being limited to sensory data, a vast realm of the unseen exists, a spiritual realm, where things are happening right now as you read these words. This realm is not some sort of science fiction parallel universe but an actual part of God's created order. We acknowledge the existence of the unseen realm every time we take the words of the Nicene Creed to our lips: "one God, the Father Almighty, Maker of heaven and earth, of all things visible and invisible."

Occupying and active in this realm are angelic beings, involved in doings affecting the world in which we live, all by God's design, operating at God's appointment. Angels are creatures, not in the sense of something grotesque or menacing, but creatures as in created beings. God created two types of beings, angelic and human, both possessing personhood and character. Angels are spiritual, unseen in their ordinary state. They are neither eternal nor all-powerful, but they are powerful and capable of activity beyond human capacity. They are everywhere present, but not in the manner of the omnipresence of the God who fills all in all, from whose presence we cannot escape (Ps. 139). Rather, they are everywhere present because of their vast number. We are told of angelic hosts, akin to starry hosts or hosts of fish that teem under the sea. In the ultimate megachurch, myriads upon myriads of angels gather in worshipful assembly with all the human saints in heavenly glory to exalt the Creator who alone is to be forever praised.[1]

Scripture suggests diversity and strata within these angelic ranks. Cherubim (singular, cherub) are stationed at Eden's entrance, flaming swords in hand. Seraphim form an angelic choir exalting God in the splendor of his holiness. Michael, one of two named angels (the other being Gabriel), carries the designation of "archangel" (Jude 9). The book of Daniel affords an extraordinary glimpse of the unseen world in which Michael is said to be in battle and one sent in response to Daniel's prayers (Dan. 10:10–21).

We're not told a lot in the Bible about the unseen realm, but sometimes the curtain is parted and we are given a glimpse, from which we draw our conclusions about angels and their purpose. Angels are depicted as messengers, guardians, warriors—all at the bidding of God, the Lord of hosts. Gabriel announced to Mary that she would be with child by the Holy Spirit. The Old Testament holds numerous examples of angels bringing messages of God in anticipation of his purpose and plans. The psalmist refers to angels' role in exercising the care of God and prompts us to wonder about the unseen reality surrounding us:

> For he will command his angels concerning you
>> to guard you in all your ways.
> On their hands they will bear you up,
>> lest you strike your foot against a stone.
>> (Ps. 91:11–12)

Hebrews 1 makes considerable mention of angels, closing with reference to their divinely appointed role as "ministering spirits sent out to serve for the sake of those who are to inherit salvation" (Heb. 1:14).

But not all angels seek to minister. The Bible describes other angels, ones who rebelled against God (Jude 6). These are called fallen angels and stand in contrast to those kept by God from rebelling, called "elect angels" (1 Tim. 5:21) or "holy angels" (Mark 8.38). Contrary to the elect angels who do God's bidding, the fallen angels, called demons, work to thwart God's purposes. Just as with any angels, demons are created beings, many in number, mighty in power, but neither omnipresent nor omnipotent nor omniscient as is God alone. And while the fallen angels in their rebellion do revel in sin and transgression of God's revealed will, they cannot help but serve the overarching plan of God that brings all things to serve his purpose in keeping with his sovereign providence governing all creatures and all contingencies (Eph. 1:11).

From this unseen realm comes our unseen adversary.

DECLARATION OF SPIRITUAL WAR

"Sin is crouching at the door. Its desire is for you, but you must rule over it" (Gen. 4:7) With those words of warning, God escorts Cain and all of us on this side of the fall onto the field of battle that characterizes life in a world under the dominion of sin, to contend with an invisible foe.

The first three chapters of Genesis set the stage for the redemptive history to follow. There we behold the eternal God, speaking into being all that is, declaring his creation "good." With the disobedience of the one man, all the created order fell under the ravages of sin. Rather than bringing down the gavel of judgment, God graciously allowed history to continue, a history that would serve as the womb for the fulfillment of his promise of a seed of the woman who would come to crush the head of the serpent.

But what would that history be like? We discover as we turn the page to the first recorded incident of a post-Eden world. The account of Cain and Abel in Genesis 4 amounts to a case study in which God alerts us to what we can expect in a world now under the dominion of sin. Sin intrudes into man's relationship with God (worship), into man's relationship with man (even the nuclear family), and into man himself where an unbridled heart of anger and pride bode ominously. Genesis 1–4 carries us from idyllic life to sin-ravaged existence, what the Bible calls "the present evil age" (Gal. 1:4), and fits us with a perspective that frames the day, puts us on guard, and calls us to arms, knowing that the days are evil (Eph. 5:15f.).

From start to finish, Genesis to Revelation, Scripture maintains this perspective of spiritual opposition to us as inhabitants of a fallen world in an evil age. Job, one of the earliest books of the Bible, provides a glimpse of this realm, not only introducing us to Satan but also surprising us with God's permission to afflict Job.[2] The veil again parts in Zechariah 3:1–5 where we witness Satan standing before God to prosecute Zechariah's sin against him.

Every New Testament writer draws our attention to the spiritual conflict that rages about us. In these profiles, God pastorally alerts us and equips us to engage the spiritual enemy. He reminds us that ". . . we do not wrestle against flesh and blood, but against the rulers, against the authorities, against the cosmic powers over this present darkness, against the spiritual forces of evil in the heavenly places" (Eph. 6:12).

Through the picture book language of apocalyptic genre, the book of Revelation reveals that Jesus Christ has won the victory and reigns on high for his church. Revelation also provides the biblical worldview and redemptive frame of reference exposing a spiritual realm and the spiritual opposition at work in what we face day by day. Not only is this spiritual opposition evident through the portrayals and prose of the book, it stands prominent at the very heart of the book and, therefore, at the very heart of life for Christ's church in a fallen world between Christ's incarnation and return in glory.

A linear reading of Revelation warms our hearts and emboldens us to press on as we move to the final chapters where the fallen order of things with their suffering and struggles gives way to the age to come, eternally unpolluted by sin. We read that and plead, "Come, Lord Jesus."

The organization of the book of Revelation, however, suggests a structure that is not linear but chiastic, directing us not only to the end of the book but particularly to its center.[3] To illustrate chiasm, consider the account of Jane's folly: "Jane went to the fair and was feeling fine. She ate too many donuts and started feeling sick. So Jane went home from the fair." Linearly, we end up with Jane sitting at home, where she can recover. But notice where chiasm brings our focus:

Jane

went to the fair

　was feeling fine

　　ate too many donuts

　was feeling sick

came home from the fair

Chiasm unfolds to draw our attention to the center and becomes an admonishment against indulging in too many donuts.

The chiastic center of the book of Revelation escorts us behind the scenes of hardship, trial, and persecution that the church and individual Christians face to reveal a spiritual foe, the devil, in chapters 12 and 13. There Satan is shown to be the monstrous god of this age, competing for people's allegiance and worship,[4] the force behind opposition to Christ and his church. As the true God is triune, so Satan is described as a counterfeit trinity, mimicking the Father by the dragon as a rival deity, the Son by the beast bearing the image of the dragon who is given authority by the dragon after the beast is healed of a mortal wound and is himself worshiped, and the Spirit by the false prophet whose role is to bring glory to the beast and who seals his subjects.[5]

Viewed in this way, Revelation stands as a pastoral book given by Christ to alert us to spiritual conflict, to assure us of his resurrection victory, and to admonish us to stand firm in what is true and trustworthy—his saving work. At the same time, it establishes us in the rigors and dangers of spiritual warfare as part of ordinary life in a fallen world, where at every turn we face opposition and obstacles, in both our walk with Christ and our work for him.

What exactly do we face in this spiritual war and how do we conduct battle against an unseen enemy? We first want to know our enemy through the profile provided us by God.

OUR ENEMY, THE DEVIL

Although forces of unseen demons infest the world,[6] God directs our attention in this spiritual realm to its leader, called Satan or the devil, to prepare us for dealing with the spiritual forces of evil. He is called "the prince of demons." Scripture accords him the lofty titles "ruler of this world" and "god of this age." Through the Bible's profile God equips us to understand Satan's intentions and tactics for the spiritual war he calls us to wage.

God's Word supplies us with a reconnaissance report on our enemy and intelligence on his tactics. The titles given him betray his character: the devil, accuser, adversary, enemy, evil one, father of lies, god, murderer, prince of the power of the air, Satan, tempter, Beelzebub, Belial, and the list goes on. Through these titles we see him as one who stands in opposition to God, his Christ, and his people. Revelation 12 portrays Satan as a dragon, "that ancient serpent, who is called the devil and Satan, the deceiver of the whole world," frustrated in his inability to destroy the male child who would rule the nations born of the woman, and so turns his fury against the church.

In Matthew 13:36–43, where he speaks of Satan's efforts against the church, Jesus both describes Satan's character ("evil one") and stance ("enemy"). Elsewhere Jesus proffers a pithy profile of our enemy:

> Jesus said to them, "If God were your Father, you would love me, for I came from God and I am here. I came not of my own accord, but he sent me. Why do you not understand what I say? It is because you cannot bear to hear my word. You are of your father the devil, and your will is to do your father's desires. He was a murderer from the beginning, and has nothing to do with the truth, because there is no truth in him. When he lies, he speaks out of his own character, for he is a liar and the father of lies." (John 8:42–44)

While Satan occupies the position of leader over the angelic demons, he also rules over human beings who by their fallen nature are part of his fallen realm. It is in this sense that

Jesus says to those who are against him, "You are of your father the devil, and your will is to do your father's desires." That means that while our enemy is not people, not flesh and blood, Satan's schemes are often executed through people still under his rule and through the principles, precepts, and practices of a fallen world. Paul speaks of "wicked and evil men" who are not of the faith but from the evil one (2 Thess. 3:2–3).[7] The world's system conveys an appearance of godliness and asserts the way of wisdom, yet through it Satan tries to lead people astray, taking them captive through hollow and deceptive philosophy and the basic principles of this world, leading them to turn away from the truth of God to myths and empty promises.

Moreover, Satan has an ally, an insider. While we as Christians are freed from Satan's grip and sin's bondage, transferred from his kingdom of darkness, in the world but not of it, there remains within us a vestige of sin. Even as regenerate beings the corruption of sin with its distorted desires remains in our flesh.[8] Upon death we will be freed from this body of sin, but for now we endure sinful inclinations and unholy desires, so that when Satan entices we find ourselves giving ear and receptivity, even if we are not responsive to the point of sin.

So we see our enemy the *devil* appealing to remaining sin in our *flesh* through the trappings of a fallen *world*. His battle rages for our mind, heart, and will, the frontlines of spiritual battle.

THE DIVINE WARRIOR

Then Moses and the people of Israel sang this song to the LORD, saying, "I will sing to the LORD, for he has triumphed gloriously; the horse and his rider he has thrown into the sea. The LORD is my strength and my song, and he has become my salvation; this is my God, and I will praise him, my father's God, and I will exalt him. The LORD is a man of war; the LORD is his name. (Ex. 15:1–3)

Here in the battle song following the Exodus, God introduces himself as the Divine Warrior, a redemptive motif that communicates the reality of a world held captive in sin and a people unable to deliver themselves.[9]

The theme of divine warfare continues the Old Testament type of God's deliverance with the people crossing the Jordan into the Promised Land. The battle to be waged is physical to be sure, but is couched in terms of holiness and is contingent on believing obedience. The old covenant sacraments of circumcision and the Passover are celebrated on the verge of physical battle, expanding our horizon to the essential nature of the warfare and pointing us to God and to redemptive realities.

In this Old Testament paradigm, not only do we gain insight into how we are to go about waging spiritual warfare, God lays out for us the basic premise for it: the battle is the Lord's. This premise comes to prophetic maturation and redemptive reality with the coming of God himself as the seed of the woman (Gal. 4:4f.), expressed in terms of deliverance:

Grace to you and peace from God our Father and the Lord Jesus Christ, who gave himself for our sins to deliver us from the present evil age, according to the will of our God and Father, to whom be the glory forever and ever. Amen. (Gal. 1:3–5)

God announces his salvation in terms of combat first in Genesis 3:15.[10] When the time had fully come, God sent his Son, the seed of the woman, to carry out this mission. How is that mission expressed? "The reason the Son of God appeared was to destroy the works of the devil" (1 John 3:8). The writer of Hebrews highlights the objects of God's mercy and the nature of the Messiah's mission with its covenantal overtones:

> Since therefore the children share in flesh and blood, he himself likewise partook of the same things, that through death he might destroy the one who has the power of death, that is, the devil, and deliver all those who through fear of death were subject to lifelong slavery. For surely it is not angels that he helps, but he helps the offspring of Abraham. Therefore he had to be made like his brothers in every respect, so that he might become a merciful and faithful high priest in the service of God, to make propitiation for the sins of the people. (Heb. 2:14–17)

After Jesus' baptism at the Jordan, which initiated his public ministry, the Spirit led him into the desert for the first step of his Messianic mission.

> And Jesus, full of the Holy Spirit, returned from the Jordan and was led by the Spirit in the wilder-

ness for forty days, being tempted by the devil. And he ate nothing during those days. And when they were ended, he was hungry. The devil said to him, "If you are the Son of God, command this stone to become bread." And Jesus answered him, "It is written, 'Man shall not live by bread alone.'" And the devil took him up and showed him all the kingdoms of the world in a moment of time, and said to him, "To you I will give all this authority and their glory, for it has been delivered to me, and I give it to whom I will. If you, then, will worship me, it will all be yours." And Jesus answered him, "It is written, 'You shall worship the Lord your God, and him only shall you serve.'" And he took him to Jerusalem and set him on the pinnacle of the temple and said to him, "If you are the Son of God, throw yourself down from here, for it is written, 'He will command his angels concerning you, to guard you,' and 'On their hands they will bear you up, lest you strike your foot against a stone.'" And Jesus answered him, "It is said, 'You shall not put the Lord your God to the test.'" And when the devil had ended every temptation, he departed from him until an opportune time. (Luke 4:1–13)

Jesus' first step in his journey to the consummate conflict of the cross involved battle with spiritual forces of evil. Jesus stood alone as the second Adam.[11] He acted as the representative of his people in confrontation with the tempter, who again issues his challenge to the directive of

God. Through Jesus' example in conducting spiritual warfare we learn of our enemy's tactics and how we might stand against them, but in so doing we do not accomplish what Christ did. The same is true of Christ's binding the strongman (Matt. 12:29). His work is not our example but our confidence, emboldening us to stand against the devil's schemes and power, for surely he has been defeated.[12]

Another way to express Christ's solitary work on our behalf is in terms of his kingdom and kingship. Christ rules now not only in the sense of creation, but of redemption. Just as Christ has always been God, but not man, so he has always been creative king, but not redemptive king, not Messianic king. In the accomplishment of his saving work, Jesus was given rule (Matt. 28:18; Eph. 1:20–22). He brought liberty to the captives. On his own, he rescued his people from the guilt and mastery of sin and the grip of the devil reflected in the power of sin.

Although Christ does stand alone as representative and champion against the devil, his dealing with temptation in the wilderness also serves as a tutorial for our instruction in the conduct of spiritual warfare. Peter refers to both Christ's example to us for our spiritual warfare as well as his unique work as emancipator from Satan's grip.

> For to this you have been called, because Christ also suffered for you, leaving you an example, so that you might follow in his steps. He committed no sin, neither was deceit found in his mouth. When he was reviled, he did not revile in return; when he suffered, he did not threaten, but contin-

ued entrusting himself to him who judges justly. He himself bore our sins in his body on the tree, that we might die to sin and live to righteousness. By his wounds you have been healed. For you were straying like sheep, but have now returned to the Shepherd and Overseer of your souls. (1 Peter 2:21–25)

Our salvation is rooted in the military intervention by our Lord, who subdued us to himself and leads us in triumphal procession, captives of his grace, in the bonds of his love (2 Cor. 2:14). When he says that he came to seek and to save those who are lost, he refers to his military mission of mercy and meekness as the promised Messiah of God.[13]

Jesus reigns on high for us, by virtue of his having been slain but now being alive (Rev. 5:5f.). He ever lives to intercede for us. As Jesus prayed for Peter against the devil who desired to sift him as wheat, he prays for our protection as well: "I do not ask that you take them out of the world, but that you keep them from the evil one" (John 17:15).

BATTLE PLAN

The pursuit of holiness to which our God calls us is waged on the battlefield of spiritual warfare. We are holy in the Lord; therefore, we are to be holy. We enjoy a positional holiness as saints of God by virtue of our union with Christ. We practice progressive holiness at the command of our God and the sanctifying work of the Holy Spirit.[14]

Paul lays out the sum and substance of our strategy for spiritual warfare in which the cardinal tenet is "the battle is the Lord's." Notice the emphasis for us in the classic passage on the subject.

> Finally, be strong in the Lord and in the strength of his might. Put on the whole armor of God, that you may be able to *stand* against the schemes of the devil. . . . Therefore take up the whole armor of God, that you may be able to *withstand* in the evil day, and having done all, to *stand* firm. *Stand* therefore . . . . (Eph. 6:10–11, 13–14a, emphasis added)

Our approach to spiritual warfare is to stand.

Standing is not passive. We don't want Beetle Bailey to come to mind. The idea is not to stand around, but to stand firm. It is to stand like an oak against the winds of Satan's lies that would sway us, against the floods of his temptations that would sweep us away, and against the leeches of his accusations that would deprive us of grace. It is to stand rooted and built up in Christ, strengthened in the faith. If our victory is in Christ, then we are to be grounded in Christ, hearing and doing his Word, living in the power of his resurrection, following his example, resting in his victory.[15] God directs us to let the word of Christ dwell in us richly, careful and alert not to be taken captive by hollow and deceptive philosophy and the basic principles of this world that is under the control of the evil one, but abiding in Christ. We are to stand firm in the gospel and the reality of Christ's librating work (Gal. 5:1), finding our strength in the resurrection power of his redemptive kingdom to which by grace we belong.

Paul's "stand" in Ephesians 6 is related to the "in Christ" of Ephesians 1, in keeping with our deliverance in Ephesians 2, in our kingdom identity and power of Ephesians 3 through 5.[16] To "stand" is tantamount to "abide" in John 15, a picture of the redemptive life and victory bound up in Christ that is ours by virtue of our union with him. "I can do all things through Christ who gives me strength"; "apart from him I can do nothing."[17] Because Christ is our refuge and strength, we are to "be strong *in the Lord . . . .*" In other words, our posture in spiritual warfare is not as maverick combatants but in solidarity with our Savior. We operate not in independent bravado, but in wisdom, humility, dependence, trust, and submission that divests us of self and invests us in Christ.

Even the armor of God's provision laid out for us in Ephesians 6:14–17 points us to Christ as it enjoins us to stand in union with him for engagement in spiritual battle. The origin of the armor finds itself in the person and work of Christ as the Suffering Servant of God, the Root of Jesse, endowed with the Spirit of God, to bring judgment on unrighteousness.

> There shall come forth a shoot from the stump of
> Jesse,
> and a branch from his roots shall bear fruit.
> And the Spirit of the LORD shall rest upon him,
> the Spirit of wisdom and understanding,
> the Spirit of counsel and might,
> the Spirit of knowledge and the fear of the LORD.

And his delight shall be in the fear of the LORD.
He shall not judge by what his eyes see,
   or decide disputes by what his ears hear,
but with righteousness he shall judge the poor,
   and decide with equity for the meek of the earth;
and he shall strike the earth with the rod of his
     mouth,
   and with the breath of his lips he shall kill the
     wicked.
Righteousness shall be the belt of his waist,
   and faithfulness the belt of his loins.
     (Isa. 11:1–5)[18]

The locus for spiritual warfare is union with Christ. All this reinforces the notion that the battle is the Lord's. In spiritual warfare our victory is in Christ; our refuge and strength are in Christ; our confidence is in Christ; our hope is in Christ. The better we learn to abide in Christ the more capable and vigorous we will be for battle as we live in and live out his victory. After describing the blinding work of Satan as the god of this age (2 Cor. 4:1–6), Paul drives home the point: "But we have this treasure in jars of clay, to show that the surpassing power belongs to God and not to us" (2 Cor. 4:7).

Spiritual warfare, whether in the work of evangelism or our walk in sanctification, can be expressed as standing firm in the gospel of the redemptive kingdom of God against the efforts of our spiritual enemy to divorce us from Christ.[19] Satan's primary efforts aim to disengage us from Christ in the gospel and pit self against Christ. Much of spiritual warfare simply involves living out that gospel of the kingdom against the efforts of our enemy the devil, with the goal of growing in the grace and knowledge of Jesus Christ. The battle lines of spiritual warfare can be drawn in terms of abiding with Christ in the gospel of grace—grace that unites us to Christ, grace that promotes our growth and fruitfulness in the strength and vigor of Christ, grace that imparts the spiritual life and vitality of Christ. It is through the battlefield of spiritual warfare that we will declare: "Through many dangers, toils and snares I have already come. 'Tis grace that's brought me safe thus far and grace will lead me home."[20]

Evidently, we are prone to forget where our strength lies. Even the apostle Paul, who makes such a ringing affirmation of it being all of God and bound up in Christ, needed God's providential prodding, ironically through Satan's effort to the contrary.

> So to keep me from being too elated by the surpassing greatness of the revelations, a thorn was given me in the flesh, a messenger of Satan to harass me, to keep me from being too elated. Three times I pleaded with the Lord about this, that it should leave me. But he said to me, "My grace is sufficient for you, for my power is made perfect in weakness." Therefore I will boast all the more gladly of my weaknesses, so that the power of Christ may rest upon me. For the sake of Christ, then, I am content with weaknesses, insults, hardships, persecutions, and calamities. For when I am weak, then I am strong. (2 Cor. 12:7–10)

The position for spiritual warfare is standing in Christ and the posture from that position boasts of weakness—our weakness that learns of and leans on Christ's victory, Christ's strength. That's why, in addressing the subject, both Peter and James call upon us to eschew pride and to humble ourselves (James 4:5–10; 1 Peter 5:6–9). The cross itself is illustrative of God's plan in battle in that it represents our vicarious victory in Christ but also points to the fundamental principle that spiritual warfare is conducted in God's wisdom and that, paradoxically, our strength is found in denying ourselves and following Christ.[21]

SOLDIERS OF CHRIST ARISE

The pages of the Old Testament abound with physical warfare. Yet even with the sword of steel prevalent in that period of shadow and type, warfare involved something more substantial, instructive for us in the battle with spiritual enemies. Along with the saints of old we can declare:

> Blessed be the Lord, my rock,
> > who trains my hands for war,
> > and my fingers for battle;
> he is my steadfast love and my fortress,
> > my stronghold and my deliverer,
> my shield and he in whom I take refuge,
> > who subdues peoples under me. (Ps. 144:1–2)

The first thing to keep in mind is that the Christian life is lived out in the context of spiritual warfare as we contend with the spiritual enemy to which our God has alerted us. A pastor asked me, "Do you ever engage in spiritual warfare?" My answer was "every day." Spiritual warfare is constituent of life in a fallen world, ordinary to the Christian life. Spiritual armor is the uniform of the day. We want to live in a state of alertness and readiness, recognizing that sin crouches at our door and its desire is for us. Our enemy the devil prowls about like a roaring lion seeking to devour, opposing us in Christian life and service. So we live, on the one hand, at peace because Christ has overcome the world (John 16:33). Yet, on the other, we live on edge and on guard, cognizant of our spiritual enemy yet confident in the victory of our Savior.

In this daily opposition, we want to live in the mindset of our redemptive identity in Christ, holy unto our God. Since we are no longer of our father the devil, subjects of his kingdom, servants of his will, we must embrace and live out our redemptive identity as children of God.[22] This identity stands diametrically opposed to our unregenerate identity and warrants a new orientation to life commensurate with that new status, freedom, power, and parentage. The apostle Paul insists on this perspective and asserts its ramifications in 1 Thessalonians 5:4–10.

> But you are not in darkness, brothers, for that day to surprise you like a thief. For you are all children of light, children of the day. We are not of the night or of the darkness. So then let us not sleep, as others do, but let us keep awake and be sober. For those who sleep, sleep at night, and those who get drunk, are drunk at night. But since we belong to

the day, let us be sober, having put on the breast-plate of faith and love, and for a helmet the hope of salvation. For God has not destined us for wrath, but to obtain salvation through our Lord Jesus Christ, who died for us so that whether we are awake or asleep we might live with him.

God has enfolded us into the visible church and given us the sacraments as a means of grace to aid us in main-taining this redemptive identity.[23] Often as a confession of faith in the celebration of the Lord's Supper I will in-clude the first question of the Heidelberg Catechism to remind us, revive us, and restore us as the church militant against Satan's opposition.

Q. What is your only comfort in life and in death?
A. That I am not my own, but belong body and soul, in life and in death, to my faithful Savior Jesus Christ. He has fully paid for all my sins with his pre-cious blood, and has set me free from the tyranny of the devil. He also watches over me in such a way that not a hair can fall from my head without the will of my heavenly Father; in fact, all things must work to-gether for my salvation. Because I belong to him, Christ, by his Holy Spirit, assures me of eternal life, and makes me whole-heartedly willing and ready, from now on to live unto him.

The Lord's Supper affirms our individual and corpo-rate redemptive identity, union with Christ, and points us to the locus of our strength. Our God spreads this table before us in the midst of this fallen world cloaked in the shadow of death, in the presence of our enemies, to focus us and fuel us in life as the people of God, situating us in the work of Christ on our behalf, and assuring us that goodness and mercy will follow us all the days of our lives and that we will dwell in the house of the Lord forever. The Lord's Supper will be celebrated only until Christ comes and for now reminds us where we stand.

We approach the table in our redemptive identity as part of the kingdom of light and life, having been rescued from the kingdom of darkness.[24] We who belong to the day are to live with eyes wide open and hearts fully inclined to our God, maintaining our focus on Christ.

SPIRITUAL WEAPONRY

The apostle Paul speaks a great deal about spiritual warfare in his epistles. We find a particular concentration in his second letter to the Corinthians.[25] That's particularly instructive to us of the real battleground when we think about the conflict in the church at Corinth with its division, sin, and errant teaching. Our enemy is not flesh and blood, and our method of war is not of this world. There Paul reminds us:

> For though we walk in the flesh, we are not waging war according to the flesh. For the weapons of our warfare are not of the flesh but have divine power to destroy strongholds. We destroy arguments and every lofty opinion raised against the knowledge of

God, and take every thought captive to obey Christ.
(2 Cor. 10:3–5)

The weapons of our warfare spoken of by Paul in this text and laid out for us in the pages of Scripture are weapons that enable us to stand and function from that stand. They teach us to abide in Christ. They operate from the posture of abiding in Christ. They serve to live in and act on that redemptive identity in Christ. These weapons of God's provision mesh with God's reconnaissance report on our spiritual enemy's character, intentions, and tactics, as we combat them in Christ.

Revealed Truth. Our enemy the devil is described as a deceiver, a counterfeiter, and a purveyor of lies, enticing us to spurn the counsel of God and inviting us to invest ourselves in his bogus offerings. God cautions us to discern between truth and error, to ingest that which will bring life rather than ruin. Spiritual warfare involves not being taken captive by the teachings of this world or distortions of God's Word but instead taking captive every thought to the obedience of our Lord Jesus.

It's noteworthy that in speaking of weapons that have divine power to destroy strongholds in the quote above that Paul goes on to speak about destroying arguments and thought that would be antagonistic to God, with the combat terminology of "taking captive" every thought to obey Christ.

We are called to discern truth from error, good from evil, right from wrong, wisdom from foolishness.[26] To be alert is to be on guard but is also to be discriminating. After speaking of the God-breathed Scriptures given to teach, reprove, correct, and train in righteousness, Paul goes on to lay out lines of battle in which this weapon is to be wielded:

> For the time is coming when people will not endure sound teaching, but having itching ears they will accumulate for themselves teachers to suit their own passions, and will turn away from listening to the truth and wander off into myths. (2 Tim. 4:3–4)

Against this opposition, along with Timothy, we are enjoined to combat these false promises and false hopes:

> Preach the word; be ready in season and out of season; reprove, rebuke, and exhort, with complete patience and teaching. . . . As for you, always be sober-minded, endure suffering, do the work of an evangelist, fulfill your ministry. (2 Tim. 4:2, 5)

The redemptive benefits of Scripture laid out in 2 Timothy 3:16–17 to equip us for every good work are exercised in the trenches of spiritual battle. The battleground is the mind, the appeal to the will, the territory in question the heart. Don't be conformed but be transformed (Rom. 12:2). Gird your minds for action (1 Peter 1:13). These are calls to battle employing spiritual weapons.

We must live grounded in the Word of God. Satan will challenge us through the sowing of doubts, the sultry whispers of sinful delight, the bully pulpits of our society, and the pundits of godless educational institutions, "Did God really say?" We are to walk in the way of wisdom, with our ear inclined to the voice of God's revealed will.[27]

This is all part of abiding in Christ. We find much the same sentiment in Colossians 2:6–8.

> Therefore, as you received Christ Jesus the Lord, so walk in him, rooted and built up in him and established in the faith, just as you were taught, abounding in thanksgiving. See to it that no one takes you captive by philosophy and empty deceit, according to human tradition, according to the elemental spirits of the world, and not according to Christ.

The issue is the lordship of Christ and whom we will follow in the battle for our mind, will, and allegiance of the heart.

Kingdom Prayer. Prayer brings us to the throne of grace for Christ's resources against our spiritual enemy.[28] Through it God grants us wisdom to discern, strength to stand firm, protection from spiritual harm, and grace to press on. Prayer as a weapon of spiritual warfare seeks the face of our Lord against an enemy that is strong, crafty, subtle, resourceful, and relentless. Such prayer is wielded in faith, faith that knows, trusts, relies on, and serves and submits to the will of God: "Your kingdom come; your will be done."

Paul highlights prayer in spiritual warfare that we might stand in Christ and find our strength in Christ. He drapes the armor of God with the overlay of comprehensive prayer: ". . . praying at all times in the Spirit, with all prayer and supplication" (Eph. 6:18a).

The prayer Jesus taught his disciples to pray in Matthew 6 escorts us to the battlefield and engages us in spiritual warfare. It is a kingdom prayer that expresses kingdom allegiance, reflects kingdom qualities, and seeks kingdom goals against the kingdom of this world. It lays siege to the kingdom of Satan in that the kingdom of God advances at the expense of the kingdom of Satan.

Our prayer is to our Lord Jesus. God does not instruct us to bind Satan with our prayer or command him to "let go" of someone in his grip. Rather, for example, we beseech our Lord Jesus to "grant them repentance leading to a knowledge of the truth, and they may escape from the snare of the devil, after being captured by him to do his will" (2 Tim. 2:25–26). Prayer seeks the power of God. As a weapon of weakness, we call upon him who is able to do more than we could ask or think (Eph. 3:20f.).

Prayer seeks refuge in Christ, who is our refuge and our strength, an ever-present help in trouble. Prayer takes its stand in Christ alone who is our strength, our rock, our fortress, our refuge, our shield, our horn, our stronghold, the one upon whom we call to be saved from our enemies. He is the one we entreat to build his church (Matt. 16:18).[29]

These images come to us from Psalms 18 and 46. The psalms are replete with warfare expression that we can employ against our spiritual foe. They provide a rich and broad arsenal for our prayer that we might stand. Psalm 46 was Luther's guide for the writing of his song, "A

Mighty Fortress," filled with expression of spiritual warfare. Try praying Psalm 46 from the vantage point of spiritual warfare. Pray Psalm 23 in light of the battle conditions of this fallen world and the provision of God from whose hand we cannot be taken as his sheep, as these truths blossom in Jesus Christ (cf. John 10).

To pray the psalms in spiritual warfare we want to remember that our enemy is not flesh and blood and our stand for victory and strength are in Christ, the subject of the psalms and the singer of the psalms, recognizing Christ stands uniquely as our champion but also conveys instruction for our combat. We want to pray the psalms from our position on this side of the cross, filling out old covenant expression with new covenant redemption in Christ.

Notice how the psalms lead us in perspective and prayer for spiritual warfare.

- Psalm 24—"the Lord strong and mighty, the Lord mighty in battle"

- Psalm 27—"The Lord is my light and my salvation; whom shall I fear? The Lord is the stronghold of my life; of whom shall I be afraid?"

- Psalm 54—"He has delivered me from every trouble and my eye has looked with triumph on my enemies."

- Psalm 46—"Be still and know that I am God. . . . The Lord of hosts is with us; the God of Jacob is our stronghold."

- Psalm 25—"O my God in you I trust. . . . Let not my enemies exalt over me."

- Psalm 32—"Blessed is the one whose transgression is forgiven, whose sin is covered. . . . I acknowledged my sin to you, and I did not cover my iniquity."

- Psalm 119—"I have stored up your word in my heart that I might not sin against you. . . . Through your precepts I get understanding; therefore I hate every false way. Your word is a lamp to my feet and a light to my path."

- Psalm 42—"Why do I go mourning because of the oppression of the enemy? . . . My adversaries taunt me . . . , 'Where is your God?'"

- Psalm 49—"Like sheep they are appointed for Sheol; Death shall be their shepherd, and the upright shall rule over them in the morning. Their form shall be consumed in Sheol, with no place to dwell. But God will ransom my soul from the power of Sheol, for he will receive me."

- Psalm 17—"Arise, O LORD! Confront him, subdue him! Deliver my soul from the wicked by your sword."

- Psalm 60—"Oh, grant us help against the foe, for vain is the salvation of man! With God we shall do valiantly; it is he who will tread down our foes."

- Psalm 121—"The LORD will keep you from all evil."

Prayer is a staple of spiritual warfare to enable us to abide in Christ, that we might stand firm and be strong and lay siege.

Covenant Community. God has not left us alone to face the foe but has enfolded us into the company of his people where we find community in the Spirit and camaraderie in mission. We need the fellowship of the brethren to watch our backs, to encourage us in battle, and to urge one another on to abide in Christ lest we grow weary and lose heart (cf. Heb. 3:12–13; 10:19–25).

The work of the kingdom is a corporate venture (Matt. 18:18–20).[30] Paul's call for prayer following his inventory of the whole armor of God for the conduct of spiritual warfare invokes not only personal prayer but also corporate prayer, not only prayer for self but for fellow soldiers in the battle to be fought and the work of the gospel to be advanced (Eph. 6:18-20).

ENGAGING THE ENEMY

Satan's tactics include deception, temptation, and accusation. He is the accuser of the brethren who prosecutes the offenses of our sin against us as we hold our lives up to the plumb line of God's law. In Christ, however, those offenses are removed from our record. By his sacrificial death, he atones for our sin. He purges our guilt. Though the sin is ours, the guilt becomes his. We are declared not guilty, not because the holy God simply pardons us, but because he pays the debt of our sin in his Son. Satan as the accuser is left without ammunition. All charges against us are satisfied in Christ.

Against Satan's tactic of accusation, we preach the gospel to ourselves, reminding ourselves of the grace in Jesus Christ that rose to bring the light of God's new creating work to dawn in our darkened hearts and that will erupt in the brilliance of heavenly glory. There we will appear before God, without fault and with great joy,[31] all because of the gospel that brings us forgiveness of sin and a perfect righteousness before a holy God. Our enemy's accusations are groundless in Christ.

Satan aims his darts at our heart. As the father of lies, he touts our self-reliance. As the accuser, he posts our transgressions. As the enemy of Christ, he promotes our rival lordship. When we look at our lives, we see sin. Doubts may plague us, guilt overwhelm us, despair sideline us, but God outfits us with the breastplate of righteousness and the helmet of salvation. We are clothed in the righteousness of our Lord Jesus Christ. Our salvation is secure in him, bound up in his accomplished work on our behalf. We engage our spiritual enemy as we *stand* in Christ's righteousness.

Our enemy is a deceiver. He tries to get us to believe and act on lies. These lies are often proffered through the world's philosophies. Hence Paul's warning that we discriminate between the teaching of the world that has an appearance of value and wisdom, and the teaching of our Lord that we are to hear and put into practice. Satan poses competing counsel to God's, counsel that will bring death, not life, and so lure followers away from the safety and security of God's truth. The devil is a purveyor of lies. Those lies are the bait for the jaws of his trap. "Did God really say?" is the first line of assault, the initial tear in the fabric of faithfulness.

Against the devil's deceptions, we are to stand firmly with both feet on the revealed truth of God's written Word. We engage our spiritual enemy as we *stand* on

Christ's truth, hearing his Word, putting it into practice, exposing error, and teaching sound doctrine to ourselves and to others.

Satan is the siren who would lure us to the rocks of spiritual ruin and impotency in Christ's service. He tempts us, playing on the sin that remains in us—the lust of the eyes, the lust of the flesh, and the pride of life. He tantalizes the lust of the eyes that sees and yearns after the world's trinkets. He arouses the lust of the flesh that indulges in anger and sexual impurity. He incites the pride of life that is more concerned for pleasing men than God, more concerned for exalting self than God, urging us to seek first our own kingdom and our righteousness, rather than Christ's.

Against Satan's tactic of temptation, grace leads us to walk by the Spirit so that we will not carry out the deeds of the flesh, pointing us to Christ:

> . . . training us to renounce ungodliness and worldly passions, and to live self-controlled, upright, and godly lives in the present age, waiting for our blessed hope, the appearing of the glory of our great God and Savior Jesus Christ, who gave himself for us to redeem us from all lawlessness and to purify for himself a people for his own possession who are zealous for good works. (Titus 2:12–14)

The Spirit who turned our hearts from idols to know and serve the true and living God continues at work in our lives, causing us to die more and more to sin and live more and more to righteousness. As children of the living God, we enjoy the full rights of sons and daughters. Our Father in heaven is disciplining us, directing and protecting us, working all things for our good that we might grow into the image of his Son in knowledge, righteousness, and holiness.

Against the devil's temptations, we are to be ever vigilant, holding fast to our Lord, finding our strength in him, girding our minds for action as obedient children in pursuit of holiness, out of love for God. We engage our spiritual enemy as we *stand* firm in Christ's strength, through whom we can do all things to which he calls us.

In engaging our spiritual foe we want to keep in place the shield of faith that fixes our eyes on Christ in all things, at all times. Jesus Christ—risen, reigning, and returning—is our surety, our shield, and our strength. And so as an expression of spiritual warfare, we stand, saying with the hymn writer:

> When Satan tempts me to despair,
> And tells me of the guilt within,
> Upward I look and see him there
> Who made an end to all my sin.
> Because the sinless Savior died,
> My sinful soul is counted free;
> For God the just is satisfied
> To look on him and pardon me,
> To look on him and pardon me.[32]

FOR FURTHER READING

Ambrose, Isaac. *The Christian Warrior*, 1660. Morgan, PA: Soli Deo Gloria, 1997.

Beeke, Joel. *Striving against Satan*. Wales, UK: Bryntirion, 2006.

Brooks, Thomas. *Precious Remedies against Satan's Devices*. Edinburgh: Banner of Truth, 1968.

Bunyan, John. *The Holy War*, 1682. Grand Rapids: Baker, 1986.

Fape, Michael O. *Powers in Encounter with Power: Spiritual Warfare in Pagan Cultures*. Ross-shire: Christian Focus, 2003.

Gale, Stanley D. *Warfare Witness: Contending against Spiritual Opposition in Everyday Evangelism*. Ross-shire: Christian Focus, 2005.

Gale, Stanley D. *Community Houses of Prayer Ministry Manual: Reaching Others for Christ through Strategic Prayer*. Humboldt, TN: Deo Volente, 2007.

Gurnall, William. *The Christian in Complete Armor*. Edinburgh: Banner of Truth, 1986.

Hanegraaff, Hank. *The Covering: God's Plan to Protect You from Evil*. Nashville, TN: W. Publishing Group, 2002.

Lewis, C. S. *The Screwtape Letters*. New York: Macmillan, 1944.

Longman III, Tremper, and Daniel G. Reid. *God Is a Warrior*. Grand Rapids: Zondervan, 1995.

Lowe, Chuck. *Territorial Spirits and World Evangelisation?* Ross-shire: Christian Focus, 1998.

Powlison, David. *Power Encounters: Reclaiming Spiritual Warfare*. Grand Rapids: Baker, 1995.

Various authors, "Angels, Demons, and Spiritual Warfare," *Tabletalk*, Orlando, FL: Ligonier Ministries, July 2007.

NOTES

1 As created beings, angels are not to be worshipped. The worship of angels is rebuked by Paul in Col. 2:18 and rebuffed by angels themselves in Rev. 19:10 and 22:8–9.

2 Satan does not act outside the pale of God's providence that governs all that comes to pass, as evidenced by Satan seeking God's permission to afflict Job or sift Peter. As Luther put it, "The devil is God's devil." The thorn in Paul's flesh in 2 Cor. 12 is described as a messenger of Satan but sent by God for God's sanctifying purposes. In parallel passages, 1 Chron. 21:1 identifies Satan as the one to incite David to sin, while 2 Sam. 24:1 reveals the hand of God in his carrying out his purpose. The word for "trial" in James 1 is illustrative. The term can mean "trial" or "temptation." God brings trials to us, but Satan is also at work. The purpose of God in the trial is our sanctification. He does not tempt to sin. Yet Satan is at work in the trial to tempt and lead us to spiritual ruin and rebellion against God. For an explanation of how Satan serves within God's plan yet rebels against his will see my book *Warfare Witness* (Ross-shire: Christian Focus, 2006), 68ff.

3 For an explanation of chiasm and its use in the book of Revelation, see Vern S. Poythress, *The Returning King: A Guide to the Book of Revelation* (Phillipsburg, NJ: P&R Publishing, 2000) and G. K. Beale, *The Book of Revelation: A Commentary on the Greek Text* (Grand Rapids: Eerdmans, 1999).

4 At its core, spiritual warfare presents a worship issue, asking whom we will honor, align ourselves with, and serve.

5 For a fuller description see *Warfare Witness*, 70ff.

6 "Though this world with devils filled should threaten to undo us . . . " (Luther, "A Mighty Fortress"). The Bible does not give us detail on the deployment of demons. If there are minions of Satan assigned to certain localities, Scripture doesn't emphasize it and certainly does not employ that concept for the spiritual conflict inherent in evangelism. Nowhere are we taught the necessity of identifying a territorial spirit in evangelistic outreach. We do contend, however, with a demonic

adversary as we would seek to penetrate the darkness of sin with the light of life. We don't want to minimize or overlook that spiritual reality for the work given to us in that dimension of spiritual warfare. This age presents us with powerful, oppressive, spiritual opposition as we move out in gospel mission.

7 See also Eph. 4:17–19 and 1 Thess. 5:4–10, as well as Satan using men like Pontius Pilate or Judas Iscariot.

8 See this ally of the evil one in our flesh described in James 1:13–15, 1 John 2:15–17, and Rom. 6–7. The particular schemes of the devil to which Paul alludes in 2 Cor. 2:11 have to do with an unforgiving spirit. The same is manifest in the spiritual battle of Rom. 12:9–21, where we are adjured to "abhor what is evil" and not to be "overcome by evil." Satan is afforded a foothold in our lives by how we handle anger (Eph. 4:26f.), often proceeding from a concern for self; this anger does not accomplish the righteousness of God (James 1:20). We want to be careful to delineate between Satan the seducer and the sinful desires to which he appeals, as well as the sin given birth to by succumbing to the temptation. It is inappropriate, misdirected, and unhelpful to demonize sins by speaking of the "demon of anger" or "the demon of greed."

9 See T. Longman III, *God Is a Warrior* (Grand Rapids: Zondervan, 1995), for an exposition of the theme of the divine warrior.

10 It is instructive to note that the promise of a Savior is spoken to the serpent rather than Adam as representative or Eve as the birthing woman. It suggests the throwing down of the gauntlet for the battle to come and the character of that battle.

11 See Paul's argument in Rom. 5:12ff., where all humanity is shown represented by two men, Adam, the first man, reflective of the fallen creation and representative of a fallen progeny, and Jesus, the second man, representative of a new creation and a redeemed people. The dividing line, the distinguishing feature between the two men, is obedience. The King of glory who humbled himself for a season would remain obedient unto death, even death on a cross. As representative of his people, his sheep given him by the

Father, Jesus would stand alone to do battle. He would be the true David, bringing victory for his people, over the Goliath of the prince of the power of the air.

12 We, individually or corporately, are not called to bind Satan or even to rebuke him. Rather, we act in the redemptive reality of Christ's work and appeal to our King who sits on the throne, reigning on high for his church. For more detail, see *Warfare Witness*, 93ff.

13 In the spiritual warfare of evangelism, we are not liberators. Christ is. We are heralds of that liberation. Christ's work is our confidence. His work says that we have something to say. We don't proclaim the possibility of salvation in Christ. We proclaim the success of his mission for his sheep. The gospel as it focuses on Christ does not offer a King who made people redeemable, but a Lord who actually redeemed his people, accomplishing their liberation. We don't fight for victory. We fight in victory, in the Lord and the strength of his might—not the might of mere divine power, but the might of redemptive power.

14 Eph. 5:8 (cf. Longman, *God Is a Warrior*, 61, for characteristics of spiritual warfare). This indicative-imperative of holiness is juxtaposed in Paul's salutation to the Corinthians in 1 Cor. 1:2.

15 Notice the emphasis of Paul's prayers in Col. 1:9–14 and Eph. 1:16–23 against the backdrop of spiritual opposition and the work of Christ as our ground, confidence, and mandate.

16 Paul arrives at the admonition in Eph. 6 by the route of God's deliverance of us in Christ, beginning with a salvation fully rooted in the triune God (Eph. 1:3–14) and realized in the victory of Christ (1:20f.); our gracious rescue from the world and its prince (2:1–7); our opposition to spiritual powers (3:8–10) as Christ builds his church; and our call to walk in the newness of Christ (4:13–20), in the light of life, knowing we still live in a fallen world (5:8–16).

17 Phil. 4:13; John 15:5. We find the same thrust in our Lord's high priestly prayer in John 17, where our oneness with Christ and not being of the world speak to God's claim on us and protection of us from the evil one as part of that claim.

18 See also Isa. 59:16–19.

19 Longman points out that Paul now applies the Old Testament language of divine warfare to "Christian discipleship and apostolic mission" (*God Is a Warrior*, 167).

20 John Newton, "Amazing Grace."

21 When the book of Proverbs contrasts wisdom and foolishness, God leads us to spiritual warfare. Will we walk in the way of wisdom, the headwaters of which is the fear of the Lord, or will we follow the way of foolishness, that which centers on self and does what is right in its own eyes? The former is the way of life, the latter the way of death—each beckoning to us. This is personified in the figure of the adulteress, who plays to our lusts and pride, luring us away from the light and truth and life of our Bridegroom. Like the song of the Sirens to Ulysses in Homer's *The Odyssey*, Satan lures, entices, and seduces us through accusation, temptation, and deception that lead us from Christ. Cf. Col. 2:8–9 with Ps. 1. The notion of idols of the heart and the challenge to faithfulness to our God carries the same tension inherent in spiritual warfare. Cf. 1 Cor. 10:12–14; 1 John 5:20f.; 1 Thess. 1:9f.; Ezek. 14:1–6.

22 Passages like Rom. 8:12–17, Gal. 4:3–9, and Eph. 2:1–7 (cf. 1:4–5 in relation to God's love and adoption) present us with a strong contrast and distinctive call as the children of God we now are.

23 The sacraments are given to the church militant. They will not be observed in the church triumphant, the church in glory. They serve to help us to stand in Christ for the work to be done. Cf. 1 Cor. 10:14–21.

24 The tension between darkness and light is a spiritual warfare concept. We are light and so we are to be light (Eph. 5:8). We are not of the darkness, so it is inappropriate for us to walk in the darkness of sin and unbelief. The light of God's truth (Ps. 119:105), the uncovering and uprooting of sin through confession (Ps. 32:5), and the openness of the accountability of Christian community (Heb. 3:12–14) are all resources of the light against the kingdom of darkness.

25 2 Cor. 2:11; 4:3–6; 6:14–15; 10:3–5; 11:14; 12:7–10.

26 See 1 John 4:1–6. Psalms 19 and 119 lead us along the same lines.

27 Notice the identical summons in Prov. 9:4 & 16, proceeding from different sources, Lady Wisdom and Dame Folly. The same challenge is laid out for us in Ps. 1, as we are called to walk in the way of wisdom and reject the way of foolishness, the way that seems right to a man but its end is the way of death. Another poignant picture is presented in Isa. 55:1–3, where the thirst of separation from the God we were created to glorify and enjoy is appealed to with water that will not quench and food that will not satisfy. The answer is to listen to God who has given his Word (Isa. 55:8–11) and delight ourselves in his covenant bounty realized in Jesus Christ as the Son of David and received through faith (cf. John 4:13f.; 6:35–41; 7:37–39).

28 For a full discussion of prayer—its resident power, its place in God's sovereign plan, the prayer of faith, praying in the Spirit, kingdom vs. therapeutic prayer, etc., see chapters 6–8 of *Warfare Witness*.

29 The dimension of spiritual warfare informs and is employed in my book *Community Houses of Prayer Ministry Manual* (Humboldt, TN: Deo Volente, 2007), a resource for equipping and involving Christ's disciples for kingdom outreach in their life-spheres.

30 Spiritual warfare is not just an individual matter. Satan's target is not just Christ's sheep but also Christ's sheepfold. Just as the individual Christian must look to retain a redemptive identity, so the local church as an outpost of Christ's kingdom must maintain a posture of militancy. John Bunyan in *The Holy War* suggests Satan's strategy to dissuade us from militancy and reduce us to a peacetime footing, the success of which is so readily identifiable to us in the church (Mansoul) today: "Mr. Sweet-world and Mr. Present-good are two men of civility and cunning. Let those engaged in this business for us, and let Mansoul be taken with much business, and if possible with much pleasure and this is the way to get ground of them. Let us but cumber and occupy and amuse Mansoul sufficiently, and they will make their castle a warehouse for goods instead of a garrison for men of war."

31 Jude's closing doxology shines all the more glorious against the intense spiritual warfare he describes in his letter.

32 "Before the Throne of God Above" by Charitie Lees Bancroft, 1893.

Also by Stanley D. Gale

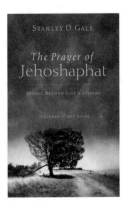

Price: $12.99
To order, visit www.prpbooks.com
Or call 1(800) 631-0094

This book develops King Jehoshaphat's prayer from 2 Chronicles 20 to give us focus, stability, strength, courage, and direction in times of great distress.

"One of the most important lessons we need to learn is how to let Scripture shape our praying. Pastor Stan Gale thoughtfully teaches us how to do that by using the prayer of Jehoshaphat."
—STEPHEN SMALLMAN

"Stan Gale is a fine guide, partner, and pastor as he directs our attention to Jehoshaphat's wonderful prayer. He sets a pace that allows us to use the prayer rather than merely know it."
—ED WELCH

New from P&R

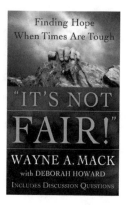

Finding Hope
When Times Are Tough

"IT'S NOT
FAIR!"

WAYNE A. MACK
with DEBORAH HOWARD
INCLUDES DISCUSSION QUESTIONS

Price: $11.99
To order, visit www.prpbooks.com
Or call 1(800) 631-0094

When people complain about their lot in life, thinking God is not treating them as he should, they need to read *"It's Not Fair!"*

"With wonderful insight and clarity, Wayne Mack explores the difficult issue of how to reconcile God's justice with his sovereignty. He shines the bright light of Scripture on some of the toughest questions of all, and then carefully explores the answers in a way that is easy to follow and truly helpful."

—John MacArthur

"A simple, yet profound and practical book. Since we are all prone to murmur against God's kind providence, everyone should read this book."

—Joel R. Beeke

Other P&R Books for the Growing Christian

Addictions — A Banquet in the Grave: Finding Hope in the Power of the Gospel (978-0-87552-606-5) by Edward T. Welch

Down, But Not Out: How to Get Up When Life Knocks You Down (978-0-87552-672-0) by Wayne A. Mack

The Enemy Within: Straight Talk About the Power and Defeat of Sin (978-0-87552-201-2) by Kris Lundgaard

Humility: The Forgotten Virtue (978-0-87552-639-3) by Wayne A. Mack

Idols of the Heart: Learning to Long for God Alone (978-0-87552-198-5) by Elyse Fitzpatrick

Instruments in the Redeemer's Hands: People in Need of Change Helping People in Need of Change (978-0-87552-607-2) by Paul David Tripp

Seeing with New Eyes: Counseling and the Human Condition Through the Lens of Scripture (978-0-87552-608-9) by David Powlison

Uprooting Anger: Biblical Help for a Common Problem (978-1-59638-005-9) by Robert D. Jones

When People Are Big and God Is Small: Overcoming Peer Pressure, Codependency, and the Fear of Man (978-0-87552-600-3) by Edward T. Welch